A LETTER OF RESIGNATION

A LETTER OF RESIGNATION

An American Libretto

Enzo Silon Surin

CENTRAL SQUARE PRESS

Central Square Press
Lynn, Massachusetts

publisher@centralsquarepress.com
www.centralsquarepress.com

Printed in the United States of America
First Edition

ISBN-13: 978-1-941604-04-5

ISBN-10: 1941604048

Cover art: "We Believed These Truths" © Enzo Silon Surin

Book design: Enzo Silon Surin

for the elders, for the next verse

to the Republic of History

I begin to vanish
feel the pull of the blank canvas
I'm contemplating that special dedication
to whoever it concern, my letter of resignation

—Black Thought "Make My"

a letter of resignation

at the brim of these lipped hours...

      silence
      split like a spine splits the body into
      hemispheres; like when the carapace splits
      and cracks in two and every other split
      is a faction, a fraction of two—like
      when the blocks busted up—an adage
      —and splits into two mothers burying sons—
      one traditionally, the other above ground
      —both eternally splitting a sum-grief
      divisible by two hands finger-split
      held and weaved like baskets,

      murder is a split-verb,
      splitting flats, flattening split-
      level townhouses into particles
      and articles of gray

why weren't we born to blanks?

the stack always sets to split:
splitting the face like cabbage
into mercurial, conjugal layers;
splitting the have-nots like lint
in a brokered pocket—hand
always reaching, hand always

leeching on
deficit, always breeching the delicate
fate that splits in two truths:
    water can swallow
    or be swallowed—

splitting the face for cabbage,
splitting the macho
splitting the macho
splitting the macho
splitting the match *yo!*—split that
wrapper, that lid for liter—
the mouth gasping for a swig of hops—

whose night won't be split like air on a lipped trumpet?

who woke the world brown-lipped?
split and read like an omen:
con-fused, cons
fusing a split cell, a split level-headedness,
splitting and splitting as we grow into a memory,
as the spine grows into a memoir and splits the body
into hemispheres into a memory,
into names we will never come
to know by heart

at the brim of these lipped hours—
we dice with glances of unrequited love
      the way within forged
      with loaded fists
      in our pockets

to fight monsters we create monsters

is that gat that goes rat attack tact tack tact tact—

is the universe city of hunger
where *the skin is dark with the stain of famine*

where the Maybach treads a trend
upon the back of our memories

is the dimness when the sounds
we make are foreign: *home is not
my own*—moan so long we hone *gone*

is the epidermis the wind splits into
factions, fractions of blue

is that fusty anthem that says:
      some are born to smile
      and we reeve that
      like a pendant

pockets full of cream
but our thoughts, still ashy

why we weren't born to blanks—

is that muffled agony
feeling like a check
praying the streets
will never cash

we wake we wake we wake—

park benches becoming a respite
for those who gurgle blood

and mornings bring
mourning to our marrow

*he ain't our child
but they all our child*

a whole day made of sulks
socks by the wayside, sobs
leading to graves

we wake we wake we wake—

at brim of these lipped hours
a mother rocks a picture frame
in her unpliable arms,
swaddling a dream:
a fatty plump of joy, whose bygone cackling
renders a primal scream
        for what
        for what was
        for what was once within her clench
        all that was once the making of a beautiful boy

        he ain't our child
        but they all our child

a loss is a loss is a loss is a—

the white lines will be stricken
from record,
street sweepers will pummel
particles of brown skin
down into cracks of tar
that the air will later refurbish

as pollen we inhale
        we inhale
        we inhale

we inhale
we in hell!

gasping on sooty air
that splits our lungs into Articles,
particles of gray

living out our days
in the milk of sadness
stroking our way
to the blocks' circumferential
edge, ever so slowly
so as not to turn this pool of fears
into a slippery mess
so as not to cause more wakes

still
we wake we wake we wake we—

free but not carefree
learning how to make trenches
every
day

brooding over whose lid won't be split
like air on the lipped trumpet?

at the brim of these lipped hours
is the postscript
of the tongue's amputation,
the mouth's round the clock succession
and street epitaph:

>   an engine's muted whirr tapers
>   and raid of revolvers disrupt
>   summer's inevitable and prodigal retribution.

is the postscript of a furious sweat
allocation of *what'evs* fosters ails—
the Avenue's blunt curves, as elegies
for young boys steadily outnumber strokes
of felt-tip pens on diplomas

is the prolongation of hands pocketed in excess,

is an addict relinquishing veins to a fraternal sponsor,

is fiber optics siphoning electricity to a vigil house,
where a mother waits for a son
whose heart is somewhere rehearsing
a non-esoteric song called *silencio*

>   weary are the days, gang-cropped and curt—this
>   valet of regress, without hesitation fails to object

to the gray matter's decapitation

when will this be the beginning of the end,
the beget that begets the cell's incessant rendition
of rebirth and reveille,
the day when noses have had enough
of the angel-dust high of evidentiary gunpowder?

at the brim of these lipped hours—
there's more than gators in the swamp
that will kill us

> *stand your ground*
> *kiss the ground*

there's something more bitter
than cold that will puncture our lungs
like bursts from a lipped trumpet:

> a lowly and dour black wallet
> a starburst mallet

there's something in the spin of our spindle
that is sifting youth like wheat—

it's treason to bury these jejune bodies—

some traditionally, the others above ground

kiss the ground kiss the ground

rat attack tact tact tact tact

splitting the macho
splitting the macho,
splitting the macho,
splitting the map, *yo!*—

why weren't we born to stints of beauty?

at the brim of these lipped hours
        drubbing is a felony—
        why aren't we all cellmates?
History's not that dumb.

economics of corroded carburetors and stalled
transmission have become a respite
for the gasping—flickers
of headlights where we once made
a trustee out of resilience, made it
habit to forgive stiff joints, now gone

the malice is in the alibis

we believe, we believe—

the ego lies, as we watch pensions
gallop toward the edge of the city
to be swallowed up in the new edition
of *How the Other Half Lives.*

at the brim of these lipped hours—
        is that unmistakably labored tone
        that separates bait from those who know it;

        that tenement-ed ever after:
        one of the begets that begat the permutation
        of *I before see*
        until it became a new fermentation;

            one of those begets that begat
            walking around with loaded fists in pockets,

            that begat some a whole lot of love
            with nowhere to putt it—*can't aim at
            a hole when you're living in it—*

is that firmament where the cool blue of lost bodies
goes *puff puff* all the way gone,

is that unmistakably labored breath that separates

bait from those who know
we were born equal
but bred as below average
     in cities of land we owned,
     land we toiled one hundred
     percent and over—very same
     places and tenements today:
     nurseries, hiding place—some cold frame with crime

    despair 'til nothing's left but to make bad
    bargains—the young among us—so reads testimony
    of causes—all who had lost connection with home-
    life or never had one, when traced back
    to the very places—at that early stage of being
    acquired—on those ships: lies lies lies of how
    the other half lived

The most was made of us while it lasted—
took to cities that stirred and grew, that soon
filled cellar to top story, with an evil
more destructive than wars

at the brim of these lipped hours
official reports read:
     they're victims of low social conditions—
     and you believe these "truths"?

this, after our necks were kept strung,
babies kept dizzied; this, after hands
were kept busy—from sun-up to sun-up.

the most was made of us while we ghosted.

how could we have known that
what would be left was to make bad
bargains or that the cheapest way out
would in time become an evil offspring;
and we, infamous ever after in our ditties?

at the brim of these lipped hours
we believed, we believed these *truths*
to be—

how many of us would make it?
we're told *hundreds of thousands* wouldn't though
millions already footed the bill—
more than a century's drift from where we once
called home—to which we are now too
often strangers—the begat vagrancy
that begat vacancy upon vacancy upon—

History's built for this purpose?

We knew how to make a look an omen
but split in level-headedness, in the settling
of scores. In fairness, how could we have known
about evil's offspring—more destructive
than wars—or being infamous
ever after in cities, earning nothing
more than interest and left to make even
more bad bargains?

at the brim of these lipped hours
               we believed—

          we believed

          these truths

          to be

          self-

          evident

     —most who had been of use
     had been used
     many of whom mistook freedom
     for free, use for living—
     were dragged again, to fields—not
     by force not by choice

still a class of tenants living hand to mouth—History's
built for this purpose. Work went on—

untold
depravities:

>*every lie has a sponsor*
>though it's clear some of us did dirt
>the history that of many of us drew dirt
>prematurely is stricken from record—a family's
>famine genealogy:

>deficit begat deficit begat deficit—
>begat terms that perpetuate a golden oldie:

>*doctor, lawyer, preacher, teacher*
>*father, mother, still, nigger*

this while our necks were kept
strung, babies kept dizzied—

>*split that cord for psalm—*

History, whose night won't be split
like air on a lipped trumpet?

at the brim of these lipped hours

we're still making a way,
but like John the Baptist, being level-headed gets us
beheaded—*spit that psalm*

for palms raised
for wails that hail a fleeting respite,
for gums split 'til they numb—

History's not dumb
but pathological:

black lives ~~matter~~ suppurate

the brown-lipped split, read
as an omen—

leveling all our best,
'cept when to glorify wrists
on the hard-court / speed
on the gridiron / eagle
on the green—just takes one
to spoil the class—

it's the result of forget-
fulness, it is one
of the ways evil has
of avenging itself

at the brim of these lipped hours—
we dream, we dream
but no one dreams this way:

no one dreams *one day I will sit on the pavement—*
the pavement of the estranged

no one dreams that a city of monuments
would be erected upon the unmarked graves
of those who braved being sold apart

oh, History!
those who don't learn
from you
                    are doomed
to repeat you   but some
profited from you—

branding demonstratively
their knock-off sonorous rants
as a new anthem—how could we
have known this evil more destructive than wars
would offspring

or that one day
a snowflake
would invade our throats

and we'd carry its exile
all the way home?

at the brim of these lipped hours
is our hour of
enter
gray
shun

is the begat that causes one brother to say to another:
> *black women are harder to love*
> *than white women*

this after centuries of harboring love in the marrow
of a bruised spine—a love toiled one hundred percent
and over—moan so long they hone groan
'til that wail out of an offspring's mouth
splits the air like a lipped trumpet

> brothers, fathers gone so long
> they mime life
> this *I gotta go and be somebody*

the beget that begat the lie:
revolution is an absentee ballot

the begat that begat the lie of our exile
we the vomit of slave ships

the truth is in the marrow of the spine
brothers in the ever after, walking around
with loaded fists in pockets—

splitting the macho
splitting the macho
splitting the macho
splitting the match, yo!

—carrying syphilitic inflictions
all the way back home

how could we have known
this absence would offspring
with not much left but to make bad
bargains?

at the brim of these lipped hours
we split
our tongues
gnashing on a glass healing

from swirling the razor blade of a horrid past

around our mouths, dubbing
we own it

this blade that seeps into the marrow of our mind
lobotomizing with lies

        the beget that begat the anthem
        there's two types of black people

the lie that begat
        A Free Can Americans
        Verses
        An other

braved the road
from split-head
in the morning
to split head
at night

we wailed we wailed we wailed

graved the load
of what was left
and parlayed the abomination
into a praise song

Obama Obama Obama
Obama Obama Obama

we wake still?
dag!
split his lid
for leader

we're free but not
care free

still a class gnawing on that ceiling
splitting our songs into a memory

this what we did before hypomnesia

this Pat Booned "we shall overcome"
coming out the mouth of history

splitting the map yo
splitting the map yo
splitting the map yo
splitting the match, yo!

at the brim of these lipped hours

betr   a   y   a   l   l

u n i m a g i n a t i v e
        ears
                    here

stray,
        cumber,
subscription to
                    mellow
                                these streets
                                come night-
                    fall's not
                    more bars,   more
windows
        but doors.
appease to
        pastoral chorus
                    of   no,
                           go,
                           slow
assemble
        migration,   for myopic

                    symbolic   climb,
dissent
                    betrayal of light,

day's

dulled out

reflection

of blades and

breath is like a perchance
of what comes naturally   to the senses—
        what comes to neighbor-
hood heap of jabbers   and mourners
concentration   of bones, of lovers
leaving   diversions
of those left between—

summer yields it gleams
traffic lights   hydrant arches stream cold
                heat's incapacitated
ritual   what comes naturally
to the make-
shift sensors   we call
love what we call   factions
                of fractions of love

the decadent equation
                multiplied by   one   shot
two
shots three shots   four
one block   new block

                                mira, pour.

at the brim of these lipped hours
we soldier on
down horrendous streets
doting the tricameral
red white and blue

don't know
which way to walk—all around us
a fresh white breaks open in a tenement.
squared suddenly into ditches, we accumulate
dust from hovering ash, skin.

seems we were just mixing stars for
passersby and blankets, for a moment

thought we could treble the sand
with songs of mortals and potters.

we weighed letters from home
on our tongues before they varied. now
a few more uses for a mouth—

one: an infinite appeal
for the torso's skeletal opus.

two: a bed for the voice's feigned coma.

three: a throated clod of dirt, to be forgotten.

we don't know which way to draw back,
waking up swiftly in a head-to-toe world
where everything is white. a renovated air
bulges with sand. we spurt in any direction.

we don't know which way to war.
so many open mouths between us,
so much crimson breaking from marrow.
the only visible road offers no access

—gone so long we home-ghost

only to be brought back home
bereft of days
bereft of nights
to face the fissures of deucalion-like floods

whose hose won't split our dome
like air on a lipped trumpet?

> *we alive but*
> *we ain't living*

a water-logged mile leads to rest stops
filled with unrest,

where an iridescent blue cannibalized the choice
of ferial days

> *sacrifice every breath*
> *I breathe*
> *To make you believe,*
> *I'd give my life away*

a fate that splits into alternate truths:
liberation
is a two-way street

at the brim of these lipped hours
is the barrel of our hue
our humiliation

in that *kept kept kept* nation
paraded in our withdrawals
for the whole world to see

flagging the bicameral
"the past is history"

thought we requited that,
that dumb other long ago

how could we have known that this evil
would offspring
and that we'd be brought back
here not
by force not by choice
with that dumb other that still prowls
in our ears without a trap?

how could we have known we'd be dragged
again or that one day we'd stumble over
something resembling a memory, wedged
in the marrow of our spine
the memoir of our first arrival?

at the brim of these lipped hours
we dot
the tees,

    blot
the eyes:

winter's
    metropolis
  pollen

etches a text-
book deluge

names
of small bright
coiled hands
weld

lead's rigid

the alluring's
blades of grass

the supple,
kowtow palm

of
summer's
streets re-   defined

we pry:
cling to lemons
for clearing

cannot tell

zipper from mouth

an ardent sting
enamel strippers

motive hater of palates

lemons always know
how to reach you

pants seams pry
open, a glare

nailing posts - affirm
graviton theory

birds can't help
dead their poses

blocks kelp don't
dead their Moses

lemons always know
how to reach you.

block disinfectants
sip c-note juice sideways

bike wheels scale
a broken torso

eye-young a crowd
creased between crisp

cracks a new brand

lemons always know
lemons always know

how to reach you.

at the brim of these lipped hours
is our rippled spit
splitting the air like bursts
from a lipped trumpet

inciting
reciting
a hello grin
as we wade
in the science
of goodbye

to pry

that exilic snowflake
from the barrel of our throat:

>   *we believe, we believe these truths to be*—no
>   we quit that—

we quit that dumb other that prowls
that winter that mellows our minds
without hesitation,
the adage that *keepin' it real* is

dicing our breath on a defiant air
courting wreckage and it's worth it,

no we quit that

we quit that dumb other without deliberation,
the benches peeled with by-gone bullets under
the direst of flight,

the syphilitic revolvers that render the block cold as mines,
paying our respects in the thug air of a mean retreat,
bereft of days,
bereft of nights,

we quit that dumb other that says
          some are born to smile

quit the trap that rendered us neutral,
noise which crows all correction is connection,

the obligatory dictation in our mouths exalting us
for our tribe-lingual amputations,

        that pillaged choice,
        that Pat-Booned our voice,

we quit noise which gleams all things correctional
as correction

that thing which causes us to hone moan
as anthem—groan so long we mime life,

we back-slash black, this what-we-did-before
hypomnesia, memory gone so long we hone groan,

we quit that unmistakably labored tone,
the umbilical hazing of our sanctuaries—

though it's clear some of us did dirt,
many of us drew dirt prematurely—our genealogy
of deficit that begat deficit that begat too many
names we will never come to know by heart

we quit History—

both bullet and barrel—
splitting our carapace like a cell splits
the body into hemo-spheres

History
both air and trumpet
splitting our cords into a memo,
read like an omen—splitting our chords
into particles and articles of refuse

we quit these lipped hours
and the perpetual sweat

while we're still standing
            and free

the masters of our own
hope and despair—

our mouths deciphering
the saline
of tears from all
other salty liquids

until You pry
that exilic snowflake
from the barrel of your throat.

Notes

1. The following text on the cover art is taken from the *Declaration of Independence of the Thirteen United States of America*:

"When in the Course of human events, it becomes necessary for one people to dissolve the political bands which have connected them with another, and to assume among the powers of the earth, the separate and equal station to which the Laws of Nature and of Nature's God entitle them, a decent respect to the opinions of mankind requires that they should declare the causes which impel them to the separation.

We hold these truths to be self-evident, that all men are created equal, that they are endowed by their Creator with certain unalienable Rights, that among these are Life, Liberty and the pursuit of Happiness.—That to secure these rights, Governments are instituted among Men, deriving their just powers from the consent of the governed"

2. Some of the content on pages 12-14 were inspired by *How the Other Half Lives,* which is a striking book by photojournalist Jacob Riis that documented the living conditions of those living in New York tenements, which were also described as New York City slums, in the 1880s.

3. The following lines *"one day I will sit on the pavement / the pavement of the estranged"* are taken from the first line in the fifth section of the poem "Eleven Stars Over Andalusia" by Mahmoud Darwish.

4. The following line *"We the vomit of slave ships"* is borrowed from *Notebook of a Return to the Native Land* by Aimé Césaire, as translated and edited by Clayton Eshleman and Annette Smith.

5. The following lines *"we alive but / we ain't living"* and *"sacrifice every breath / I breathe / To make you believe, / I'd give my life away"* are taken from Cee-Lo Green's verse in the song "Liberation" by Outkast, featuring Erykah Badu, Big Rube & Cee-lo.

6. Pat Boone was a rock and roll singer and one of many white artists during the 1950s and 1960s who built their careers recording covers of songs originally performed by black artists. He famously released a cover of Little Richard's *"Tutti Frutti"* and consequently surpassed Richard's original version on the pop charts. Although cover songs were standard industry practice in that era, these alternate versions said more about the racial attitude of the country since white mainstream radio stations would not play music by black artists.

about the author

Enzo Silon Surin is a Haitian-born poet, educator, publisher and social advocate. He is the author of two chapbooks, *A Letter of Resignation* (2017) and *Higher Ground* (2006), which was nominated for the Massachusetts Book Award and co-author of The Next Verse Poets Mixtape - Volume One: the 4 X 4 (2016). His poetry has been featured in *Interviewing the Caribbean, Pangyrus, jubilat, Soundings East, The BreakBeat Poets: New American Poetry in the Age of Hip-Hop, Naugatuck River Review, sx salon*, and *Tidal Basin Review,* among others. He was recognized as the 2015 PEN New England Celebrated New Voice in Poetry and his manuscript, *When My Body Was a Clinched Fist*, was selected as a semi-finalist for the 2015 Philip Levine Poetry Book Prize. Surin holds an MFA in Creative Writing from Lesley University and is currently Associate Professor of English at Bunker Hill Community College and founding editor and publisher at Central Square Press.

CPSIA information can be obtained
at www.ICGtesting.com
Printed in the USA
BVOW06s2052200817
492610BV00004B/6/P